Thoughts and Feelings

Thoughts and Feelings

Thanks

Written by Ruth Shannon Odor
Photos by David M. Budd

The Child's World®, Inc.

Published by The Child's World®, Inc.

Copyright © 2000 by The Child's World®, Inc.
All rights reserved. No part of this book may be
reproduced or utilized in any form or by any means
without written permission from the publisher.
Printed in the United States of America.

Design and Production:
The Creative Spark, San Juan Capistrano, CA

Photos: © 1998 David M. Budd Photography

Library of Congress Cataloging-in-Publication Data

Odor, Ruth Shannon, 1926–
       Thanks / by Ruth Shannon Odor.
          p. cm. -- (Thoughts and Feelings)
       Includes bibliographical references.
       Summary: Simple rhyming text describes the importance of feeling
    thankful and some situations in which it is appropriate to say,
    "Thanks."
       ISBN 1-56766-667-9 (lib.bdg. : alk. paper)
       1. Gratitude in children Juvenile literature. [1. Gratitude.
     2. Etiquette.]   I. Title. II. Series.
    BF723.G7036   1999
    395.1'22--dc21   99-28174
                                                               CIP

THANKS.

It's a feeling I have, and
a word that I say—
not just now and then,
but most everyday.
It means I'm glad and
I'm thankful too,
for the things people give me,
and the things that they do.

7

My mom cooks food for
the whole family,
but sometimes something
especially for me.

9

10

The food that she makes
always tastes really good.
I say, "Thanks, Mom!"
because I know that I should.

Although Dad is tired
at the end of the day,
he picks me right up and says,
"Come on, let's play!"

We have so much fun,
whenever we play.

14

"Thanks, Dad," I always remember to say.

On my last birthday,
I got a neat new toy.
It's a special thing,
something I really enjoy!
As I opened it up,
I remembered to say,
"Thank you!
This is a really good day!"

At school I have problems
writing my name,
or remembering the rules to
some silly game.

My teacher's right there.
She's really nice, you see.
"Thanks, Teacher," I say.
"Thanks for helping me."

"Hey, I have some candy!"
says my friend Mike.
I see that it's cherry,
just the kind that I like!
He gives me a piece;
I thought that he would.
"Thanks, Mike.
This candy is really good!"

Sometimes I get sad,
or a little bit blue.
My mom always knows
just what to do.
She gives me a hug
and says its OK.

"You're great, mom. Thanks,"
I remember to say.

My uncle comes over
and talks to me.
He is a very good
friend, you see.

27

We spend time together,
there's so much to do.
I'm glad and I say,
"Hey, Uncle David,
thank you!"

When you are glad,
and grateful too,
for the things people give you,
and the things that they do,

"THANKS"

is just the right word to say—
not just now and then,
but most every day.

31

For Further Information and Reading

Books

Hayes, Wanda. *Saying Thank You Makes Me Happy.* Standard Publishing, 1994.

Polacco, Patricia. *Thank You, Mr. Falker.* NY: Philomel Books, 1998.

Scarry, Richard. *Richard Scarry's Please and Thank You Book.* New York: Random House, 1990.

Web Sites

For information about thoughts and feelings:
http://www.kidshealth.org/kid/feeling/

Fairy tales and stories about thoughts and feelings from all over the world: http://www.familyinternet.com/StoryGrowby/